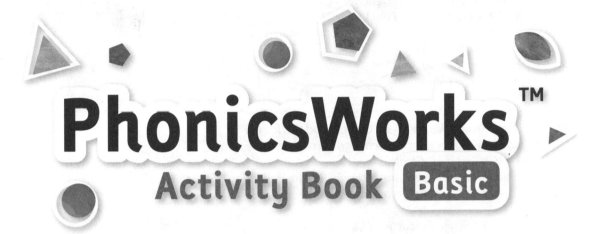

PhonicsWorks™
Activity Book Basic

Book Staff and Contributors

Kristen Kinney   *Director, Primary Literacy*
Lenna King, Amy Rauen   *Instructional Designers*
Mary Beck Desmond   *Senior Text Editor*
Jill Tunick   *Text Editor*
Suzanne Montazer   *Creative Director, Print and ePublishing*
Jayoung Cho   *Senior Print Visual Designer*
Jacqueline E.P. Rosenborough   *Print Visual Designer*
Kim Barcas, Stephanie Shaw Williams   *Cover Designers*
Amy Eward   *Senior Manager, Writers*
Susan Raley   *Senior Manager, Editors*
Deanna Lacek   *Project Manager*

Maria Szalay   *Executive Vice President, Product Development*
John Holdren   *Senior Vice President, Content and Curriculum*
David Pelizzari   *Vice President, Content and Curriculum*
Kim Barcas   *Vice President, Creative*
Laura Seuschek   *Vice President, Instructional Design, Evaluation & Studies*
Aaron Hall   *Vice President, Program Management*

Lisa Dimaio Iekel   *Senior Production Manager*

Illustrations Credits
All illustrations © K12 unless otherwise noted

About K12 Inc.
K12 Inc. (NYSE: LRN) drives innovation and advances the quality of education by delivering state-of-the-art digital learning platforms and technology to students and school districts around the world. K12 is a company of educators offering its online and blended curriculum to charter schools, public school districts, private schools, and directly to families. More information can be found at K12.com.

978-1-60153-125-4
Printed by Bradford & Bigelow, Newburyport, MA, USA, July 2020,

Contents

Sounds /m/ and /t/

The Beginning

Circle pictures whose name begins with the sound /m/.
Draw an X over pictures whose name begins with the sound /t/.

Sounds /n/ and /p/
The Beginning

Circle pictures whose name begins with the sound /p/.
Draw an X over pictures whose name begins with the sound /n/.

Sounds /ē/ and /h/
The Beginning

Circle pictures whose name begins with the sound /h/.
Draw an X over pictures whose name begins with the sound /ē/.

Sounds /d/ and /ŏ/

Sound Search

Circle pictures whose name ends with the sound /d/.
Draw an X over pictures whose name has the sound /ŏ/.

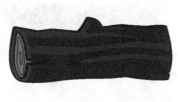

Sounds /b/ and /f/
The Beginning

Circle pictures whose name begins with the sound /b/.
Draw an X over pictures whose name begins with the sound /f/.

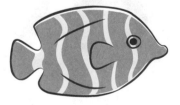

Sound /ā/

Sound Search

Circle pictures whose name has the sound /ā/.

Sounds /g/ and /ō/
Sound Search

Circle pictures whose name ends with the sound /g/.
Draw an X over pictures whose name has the sound /ō/.

Sound /j/
Same Sound

In each row, circle pictures whose name begins with the same sound.

Sound /s/
The Beginning

Circle pictures whose name begins with the sound /s/.

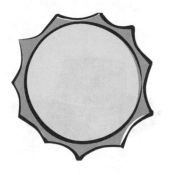

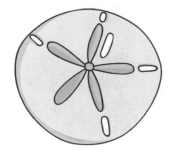

Sounds /ă/ and /w/
Sound Search

Circle pictures whose name has the sound /ă/.
Draw an X over pictures whose name has the sound /w/.

Sounds /z/ and /ī/

Sound Search

Circle pictures whose name has the sound /z/.
Draw an X over pictures whose name has the sound /ī/.

Sound /l/

Same Sound

In each row, circle pictures whose names begin with the same sound.

PHONICS

Try It

Sounds /th/ and /th/
The Beginning

Circle pictures whose name begins with the sound /th/.

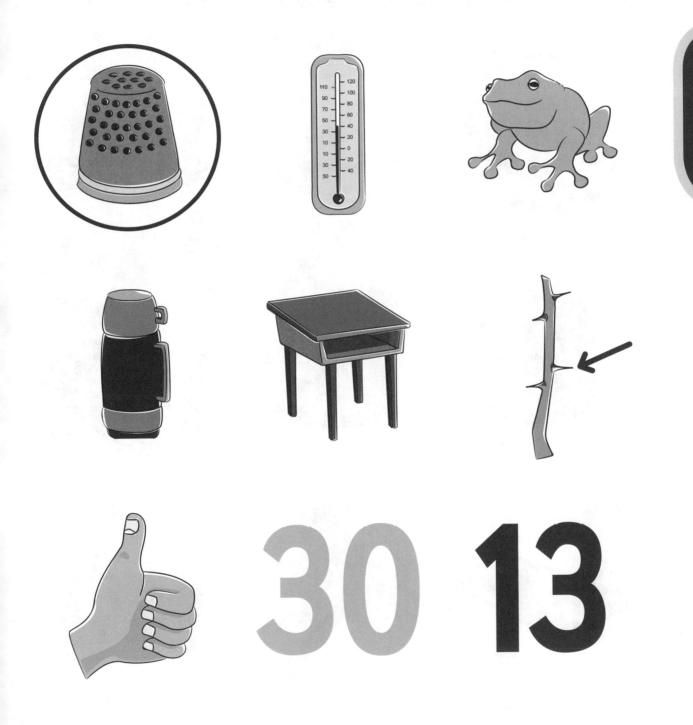

Sounds /ĕ/ and /k/
Sound Search

Circle pictures whose name has the sound /k/.
Draw an X over pictures whose name has the sound /ĕ/.

Sound /v/

Sound Search

Circle pictures whose name has the sound /v/.

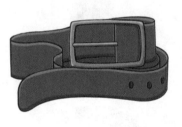

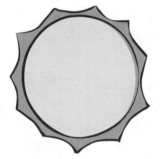

Sound /r/
The Beginning

Circle pictures whose name begins with the sound /r/.

Sound /ĭ/

Sound Boxes

Color the first box if the word begins with the sound /ĭ/.
Color the middle box if the sound /ĭ/ is in the middle of the word.

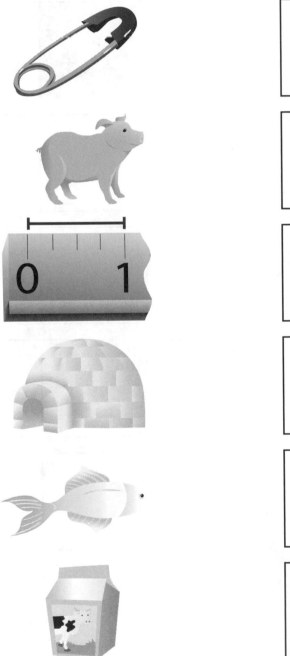
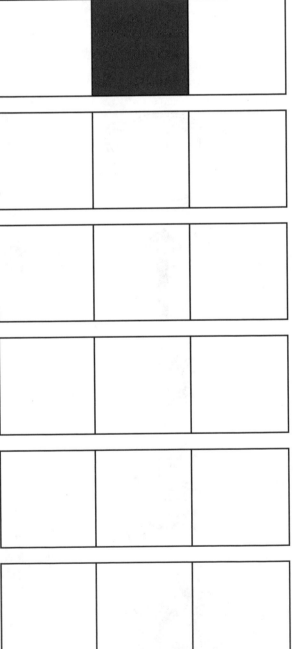

Sound /ŭ/

Sound Boxes

Color the first box if the word begins with the sound /ŭ/.
Color the middle box if the sound /ŭ/ is in the middle of the word.

PHONICS

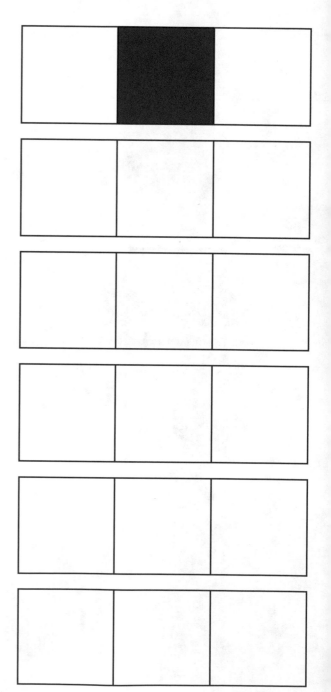

Sound /ch/

Sound Boxes

Color the first box if the word begins with the sound /ch/.
Color the end box if the sound /ch/ is at the end of the word.

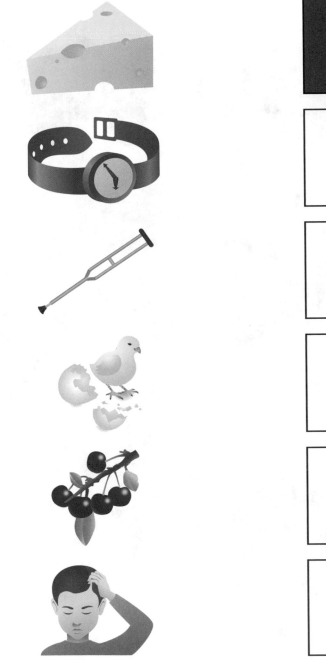

Sound /y/
The Beginning

Circle pictures whose name begins with the sound /y/.

Sound /sh/

The Beginning

Circle pictures whose name begins with the sound /sh/.

Sound /aw/

Sound Search

Circle pictures whose name has the sound /aw/.

Sound /kw/

The Beginning

Circle pictures whose name begins with the sound /kw/.

Syllables and Sounds
Careful Counting

Count the number of syllables you hear.

PHONICS

_____

_____

_____

_____

_____

_____

Sound /oi/
Sound Search

Circle pictures whose name has the sound /oi/.

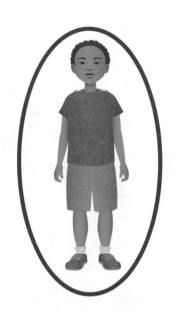

Sound /ū/

The Beginning

Circle pictures whose name begins with the sound /ū/.

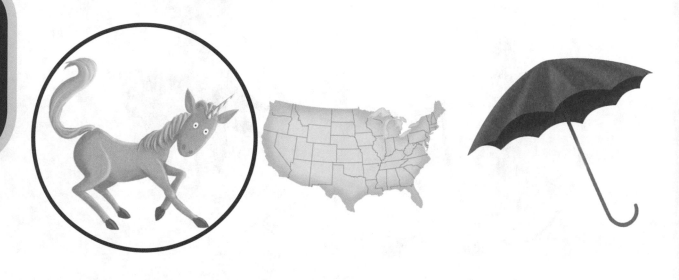

Sound /ks/

The End

Circle pictures whose name ends with the sound /ks/.

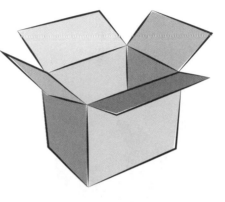

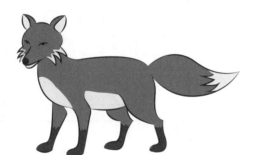

Sound Practice

Sound Boxes

As you say a sound, color a box using a new color for each sound.

Long Double *o* Sound
Sound Search

Circle pictures whose name has the sound /o͞o/.

Sound /ow/
Sound Search

Circle pictures whose name has the sound /ow/.

PHONICS

Sound Practice (A)
Sound Search

Circle pictures whose name has the sound /o͞o/.

Sound Practice (B)
Guide Words

Say the name of the picture. Say the vowel sound as you color the picture. Say a word that has the same beginning sound.

PHONICS

apple

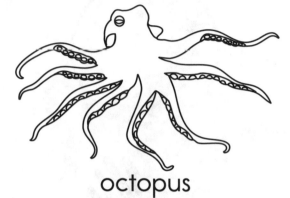

octopus

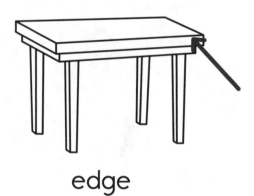

edge

itch

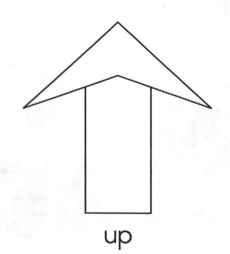

up

Sounds for Letters *a*, *m*, *s*, and *t*
Reading Practice

Touch and read each word aloud.

sat	mat
mat	at
sat	the
is	and

Read the sentence aloud. Color the picture.

The cat is at the mat.

Sounds for Letters *c* and *h*
New Beginnings

Circle the beginning letter of the picture name. Write the beginning letter to make the word. Read the word aloud.

j or (c)? ____c____ at

b or s? _____ at

f or h? _____ at

m or t? _____ at

Sounds for Letters *l* and *n*
Reading Practice

Touch and read each word aloud.

lab	can
fan	on
to	man
in	cab

Read the sentence aloud. Color the picture.

Jan is in the lab.

Review Sounds for Letters

Rhyme Time

Circle the word under the sentence that rhymes with
the underlined word. Write the word.

1. The man has a <u>cat</u>. The cat is _____ **fat** _____.

   fan   (fat)

2. Jan has a <u>pan</u>. The pan is _____.

   tan   lap

3. Sam ran a <u>lap</u>. Sam had to _____.

   jam   nap

4. Pam has the <u>ham</u>. Sam has the _____.

   jam   nab

Sound for Letter *o*

Finish the Job

Choose a word from the box to complete the sentence.
Write the word. Read the sentence aloud.

pot	job
hop	Mom

1. The ham is in the _____.

2. Tom can _____.

3. Bob has a _____.

4. _____ has the jam.

Sounds for *k* and *v*

Rhyme Time

Circle the word under the sentence that rhymes with the underlined word. Write the word.

1. Mom has a <u>van</u>. It is ___**tan**___.

   (tan)   fat

2. Bob is <u>hot</u>. He has a _____.

   pot   pan

3. It is <u>Kat</u>. Kat is on a _____.

   van   mat

4. This is a <u>vat</u>. The vat is _____.

   hot   fat

Getting Stronger: Sounds /ă/ and /ŏ/ (A)

Go Fish!

Color fish with the sound /ă/ pink. Color fish with the sound /ŏ/ yellow.

top

cab

gap

bag

jot

gas

Getting Stronger: Sounds /ă/ and /ŏ/ (C)
Different Beat

Read each word in the row aloud. Circle the word in the row that does **not** rhyme with the others.

1. ram   jam   (mom)   ham

2. pot   dog   fog   hog

3. can   tan   log   pan

4. hop   pop   top   jog

5. job   rob   sob   dot

PHONICS

Introduce Sounds for Letters *i*, *qu*, and *z*
Go Fish!

Color fish with the sound /ĭ/ pink. Color fish with the sound /ŏ/ yellow.

Practice Sounds for Letters *i, qu,* and *z* (B)
Different Beat

Read each word in the row aloud. Circle the word in the row that does **not** rhyme with the others.

1. big   pig   (kit)   fig

2. quit   sit   him   pit

3. hip   bib   rib   fib

4. Kim   pop   rim   dim

5. quiz   tin   pin   fin

Getting Stronger: Sounds /ă/, /ĭ/, and /ŏ/ (A)
Yes or No?

Look at the picture. Read the question. Write *Yes* or *No*.

Yes or No

1. Is the fan in the can? _____

2. Is the cat on the mat? _____

3. Is the tot sad? _____

4. Is the dog big? _____

Getting Stronger: Sounds /ă/, /ĭ/, and /ŏ/ (C)
To the Rescue

Help the rabbit find the path to the log.
Color the boxes that name real words.

jam	nod	zil
mip	did	taf
lod	quit	dal
boj	hat	fif
quan	dot	zat
gor	pig	kol

Introduce Sounds for Letters *u*, *w*, and *x*

Finish the Job

Choose a word from the box to complete the sentence.
Write the word. Read the sentence aloud.

bus	fun
hut	wax

1. The _____ has six kids on it.

2. The _____ is hot.

3. Bud is in the _____.

4. He had _____ in the sun.

Practice Sounds for Letters *u*, *w*, and *x* (B)
Scrambler

Unscramble the letters to create a word. Write the word.
Read the word aloud.

PHONICS

1. x f o _____

2. n f u _____

3. c p u _____

4. a x w _____

Getting Stronger: Sounds /ă/, /ĭ/, /ŏ/, and /ŭ/ (A)

The Amazing Alphabet

Circle the letter that makes the vowel sound in the picture name. Write the letter. Say the name.

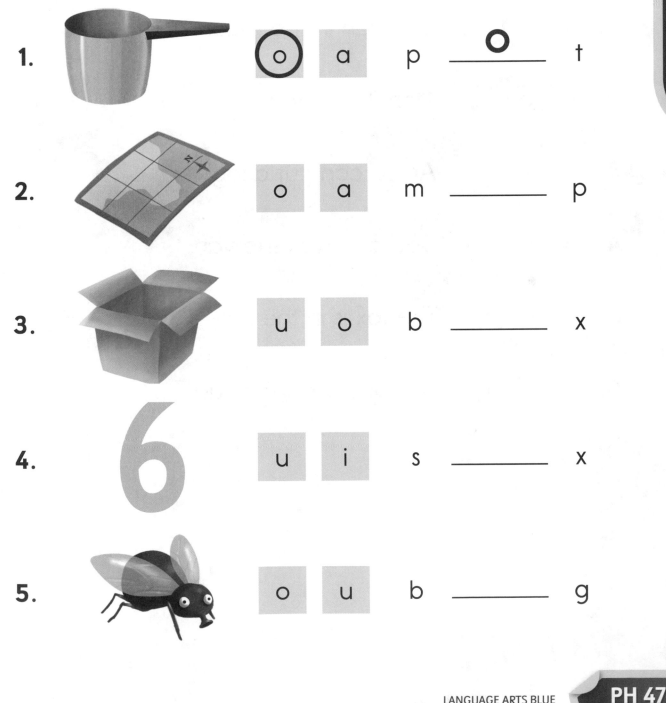

1. ⭕o a   p ___o___ t

2. o a   m _____ p

3. u o   b _____ x

4. u i   s _____ x

5. o u   b _____ g

Getting Stronger: Sounds /ă/, /ĭ/, /ŏ/, and /ŭ/ (C)

Short Vowels

Read the word aloud. Circle the short vowel.
Then read the sentence aloud.

1. m (u) d   Mac ran in the mud.

2. f a n   Mom has a fan.

3. a x   An ax can cut a log.

4. w a x   Dad can wax the van.

5. f o x   The fox is in the log.

6. r u g   The pup is on the rug.

Introduce Sounds for Letters *e* and *y*

Go Fish!

Color fish with the sound /y/ pink. Color fish with the sound /ĕ/ yellow.

Practice Sounds for Letters *e* and *y* (B)

Mixed Up

Read the row of mixed-up words aloud. Unscramble the words and write a sentence.

Clue: The word that begins with a capital letter goes first.

1. The vet wet. got

_____

2. hen. the Get red

_____

3. yet? Ben Is ten

_____

PHONICS

Try It

Getting Stronger: Sounds /ă/, /ĕ/, /ĭ/, /ŏ/, and /ŭ/ (A)

The Amazing Alphabet

Circle the letter that makes the vowel sound in the picture name. Write the letter. Say the name.

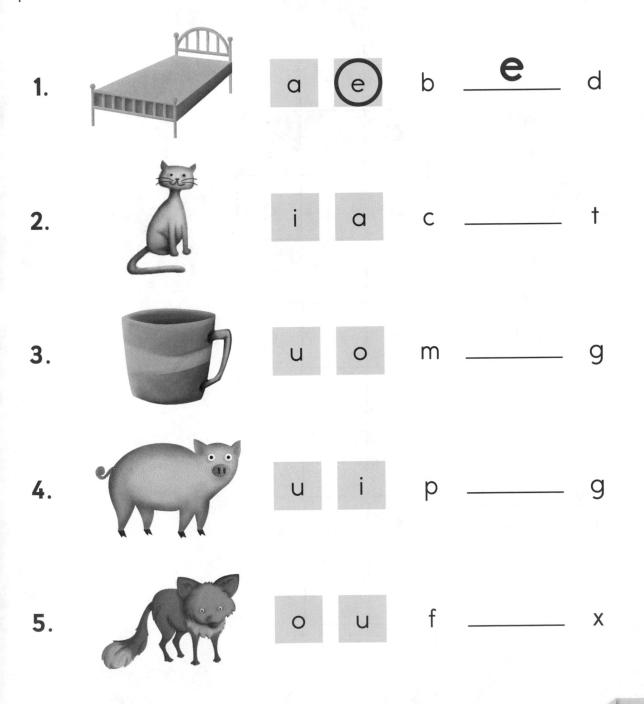

1.   a   (e)   b   __e__   d

2.   i   a   c   _____   t

3.   u   o   m   _____   g

4.   u   i   p   _____   g

5.   o   u   f   _____   x

PHONICS

Getting Stronger: Sounds /ă/, /ĕ/, /ĭ/, /ŏ/, and /ŭ/ (C)

Word Chains

One letter has been changed to make the next word.
Color the box that has the changed letter.

b	e	t
b	e	g
b	u	g
b	i	g
w	i	g
w	i	n
f	i	n
f	i	x
m	i	x

Review Short Vowels (A)

Alphabet Addition

Add the letters to make a word. Write the word, and then read it aloud.

1. c + at = _____ cat _____

2. m + at = _____

3. f + it = _____

4. s + it = _____

5. b + us = _____

6. D + on = _____

.Just for Fun···

Read the silly sentence.

The fat cat did not fit in the bus.

PHONICS

Review Short Vowels (C)

Dissect It

Circle the vowel. Read the word aloud, and then write the word.

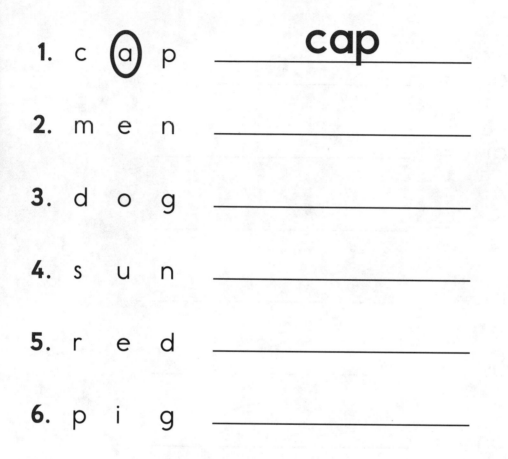

1. c (a) p   cap _____

2. m e n   _____

3. d o g   _____

4. s u n   _____

5. r e d   _____

6. p i g   _____

PHONICS

Getting Stronger: Short Vowels (A)
Such Nonsense

Read the group of words. The word that is underlined is a nonsense word. How would you say it? What could it mean?
Draw a picture to go with the word.

a wet <u>zet</u>

a red <u>ged</u>

a <u>ret</u> in a net

a hen and a <u>nen</u>

Getting Stronger: Short Vowels (C)
To the Rescue

Help the rabbit find the path to the log.
Color the boxes that name real words.

red	yev	gol
beg	yet	bap
yit	pen	tax
zug	coj	set
yim	yes	win
pij	jug	sof

Introduce Digraph *sh*

Picture This

Fill in the blank with the digraph *sh*. Then read the word aloud.

sh ___ ip

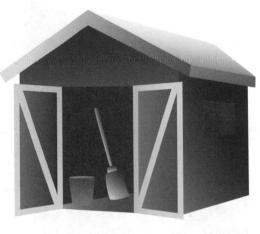

_____ ed

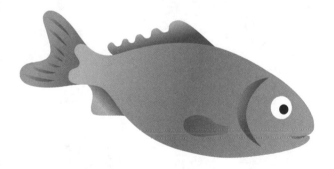

fi _____

di _____

PHONICS

Introduce Digraph *th*
Go Fish!

Color fish with the sound /sh/ yellow. Color fish with the sound /th/ pink.

PHONICS

Getting Stronger: Short Vowels (A)
Word Chains

One or two letters have been changed to make the next word.
Color the box that has the changed letter or letters.

b	a	sh
c	a	sh
d	a	sh
d	i	sh
w	i	sh
w	i	g
w	a	g
t	a	g
t	u	g
m	u	g

Getting Stronger: Digraphs (A)
To the Rescue

Help the rabbit find the path to the log.
Color the boxes that name real words.

thin	thab	hith
this	bath	thid
thig	them	thud
thun	thip	math
thap	moth	than
quith	then	yath

LANGUAGE ARTS BLUE

Introduce Digraph *wh*
Identification, Please

Read the word part or letter aloud. Circle the digraphs *wh*, *sh*, and *th*.

had–	sh)og–	shun–	whis–	whap–
w	l	y	qu	x
whog–	whum–	–ath	–eth	–ith
e	i	o	u	a
–ash	whesh–	–ush	–esh	–oth

Introduce Digraph *ch*
Sorting Day

Color *wh* words blue. Color *ch* words pink.

chip	much	rich	chop
such	whip	whiz	chap
chug	chum	Chad	chin

Getting Stronger: Letter Sounds (A)
Word Chains

One or two letters have been changed to make the next word.
Color the box that has the changed letter or letters.

p	e	n
wh	e	n
m	e	n
m	e	t
m	a	t
th	a	t
ch	a	t
ch	a	p
ch	i	p
sh	i	p

Getting Stronger: Letter Sounds (C)
Hunt for Information

Choose a word from the story that completes the sentence. Write the word.

> Dad got Pam a cat. He got it at the pet shop. Pam and the cat have such fun. So Pam is not sad. The cat is a chum for Pam.

1. Dad got a _____ **cat** _____ for Pam.

2. The cat was at the _____ shop.

3. Pam has _____ with the cat.

4. Pam is not _____.

5. The cat is Pam's _____.

Introduce Trigraph *tch*

Different Beat

Read each word in the row aloud. Circle the word in the row that does **not** rhyme with the others.

1. (can)   ditch   pitch   hitch

2. witch   catch   Mitch   itch

3. batch   match   Man   latch

In order, write each word you circled on the blank lines in the sentence. Read the sentence aloud.

4. You _____ not _____

   me, I'm the Gingerbread _____ .

Introduce Ending –*ck*

Match It

Read the words in the first column aloud. Read the words in the second column aloud. Draw a line to match the words that rhyme.

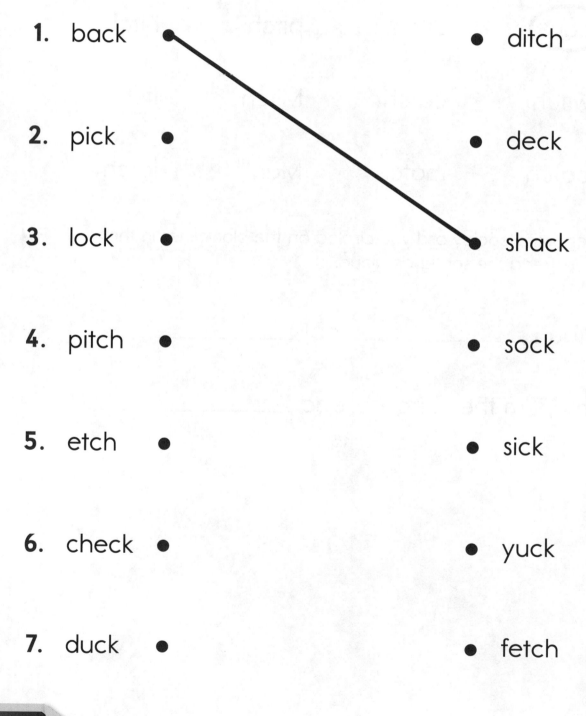

1. back   ditch

2. pick   deck

3. lock   shack

4. pitch   sock

5. etch   sick

6. check   yuck

7. duck   fetch

Getting Stronger: Digraphs *ch*, *sh*, and *th*

Alphabet Addition

Add the letters to make a word. Write the word, and then read it aloud.

1. d + ish = _____dish_____

2. s + ash = _____

3. ch + ug = _____

4. th + ick = _____

5. p + ath = _____

6. m + uch = _____

Getting Stronger: Review Digraphs, Ending –ck, and Trigraph tch (A)

Sorting Day

Color animal words yellow. Color other words red.

chick	ship	lock	hog
fish	dish	duck	match
yak	chip	buck	patch

Review Digraphs and Trigraphs (A)
Alphabet Addition

Add the letters to make a word. Write the word, and then read it aloud.

1. c   +   atch=   **catch** _____

2. f   +   etch= _____

3. M   +   itch = _____

4. ch +   ick   = _____

5. b   +   ack = _____

6. r   +   ock = _____

🌙 **Just for Fun**

Read the silly sentences.

Can a chick catch a rock?

Can a rock catch a chick?

PHONICS

Review Digraphs and Trigraphs (C)
New Endings

Circle the ending letter or letters, and write them on the line. Read the word aloud.

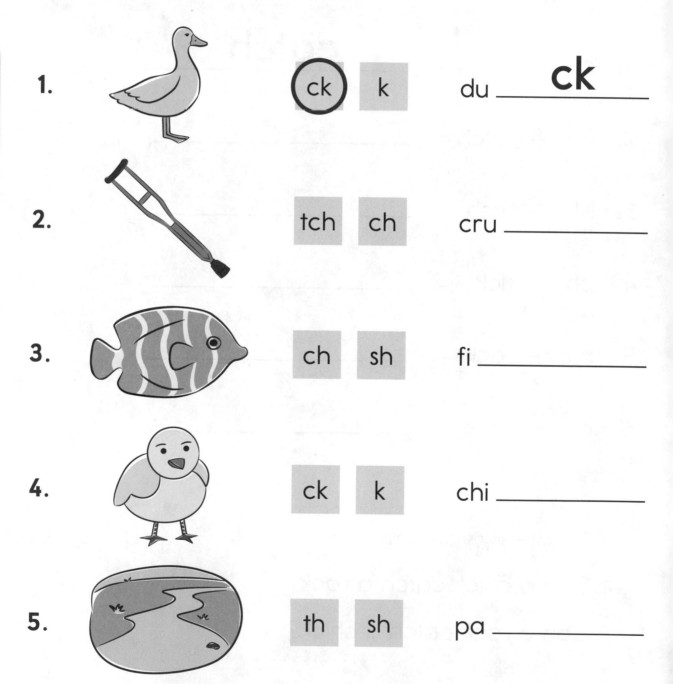

1. (ck) k   du ___**ck**___

2. tch   ch   cru _____

3. ch   sh   fi _____

4. ck   k   chi _____

5. th   sh   pa _____

Getting Stronger: Digraphs and Trigraphs (A)
Word Chains

One or two letters have been changed to make the next word. Color the box that has the changed letter or letters.

c	a	tch
h	a	tch
m	a	tch
p	a	tch
l	a	tch
b	a	tch
b	a	ck
r	a	ck

l	a	ck
s	a	ck
qu	a	ck
qu	i	ck
ch	i	ck
ch	e	ck
n	e	ck

Getting Stronger: Digraphs and Trigraphs (C)

Hunt for Information

Choose a word from the story that completes the sentence. Write the word.

> Jack is at the dock to fish. Jack has bad luck. He can catch a fish. But he cannot catch a batch of fish.

1. Jack is at the __**dock**__.

2. Jack can _____ at the dock.

3. Jack has _____ luck.

4. Jack can catch _____ fish.

5. He cannot catch a _____ of fish.

Capitalize Sentences

Just Right!

On the first line, rewrite the first word with a capital letter.
On the second line, put a period. Read the sentence aloud.

1. the _____**The**_____ man put the box

   in the shed __•__

2. jen _____ has a rash on

   her back ____

3. chop _____ the log with

   that ax ____

4. we _____ have hot dogs

   and chips ____

5. dash _____ up the path to

   the shed ____

Create Sentences

Just Right!

Put a question mark at the end of the sentence.
Read the sentence aloud.

1. Did Sam catch a big fish __?__

2. When did Mom fix that box ____

3. Did you chop the log ____

4. Can you do your math ____

5. Is your chick in the shed ____

6. Did you wish for a lot of cash ____

Getting Stronger: Short Vowels
Best Pick

Read the sentence aloud and circle the word that best completes it.
Then write the word.

1. I can ___**run**___ up the path.

2. Did the cat get _____?

3. Dad had a _____.

4. Can you _____ my hat?

5. The dog can _____.

bud	(run)
mad	mud
bath	jam
bus	get
cat	yip

Getting Stronger: Capitalize and Punctuate Sentences

Just Right!

On the first line, rewrite the first word with a capital letter.
On the second line, put a period. Read the sentence aloud.

1. chad _____Chad_____ did not pick the

    fish for a pet __.__

2. rick _____ went with her to

    the dock ____

3. i _____ see you have a

    quiz in math ____

4. she _____ got the job ____

5. the _____ chick and the hen

    can peck ____

Introduce Ending –s
Alphabet Addition

Add the letters to make a word. Write the word, and then read it aloud.

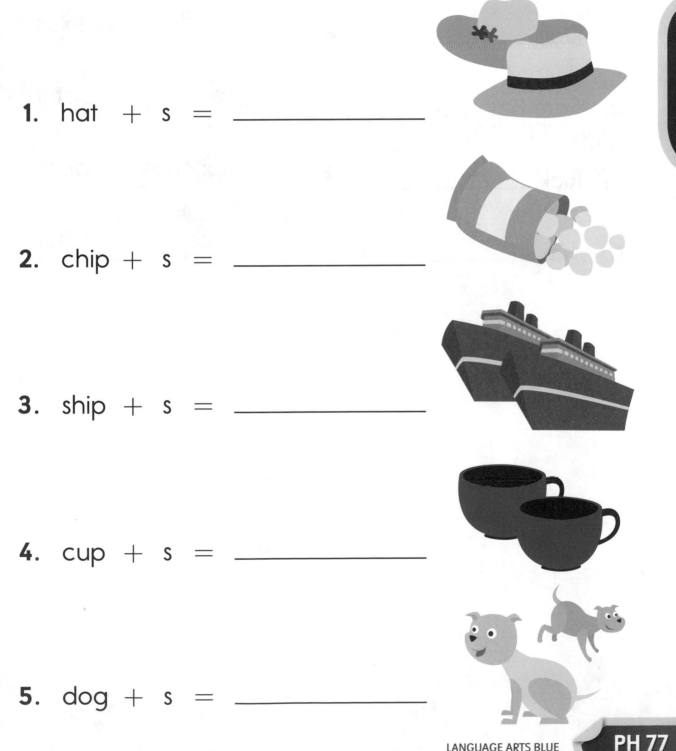

1. hat + s = _____

2. chip + s = _____

3. ship + s = _____

4. cup + s = _____

5. dog + s = _____

Introduce Ending –es

Best Pick

Read the sentence aloud and circle the word that best completes it. Then write the word.

PHONICS

1. Dad _____ the van.

2. Sam has two _____.

3. Rick _____ to Sam.

4. Kim _____ ten fish.

fix	fixes
patches	patch
pitches	pitch
catches	catch

Getting Stronger: Vowels (A)
By Sight

Reading across the rows, see how many words you can read correctly in one minute. When you get to the bottom of the page, start over.

one	her	or	so	want
we	both	put	there	with
why	she	with	your	their
went	the	of	from	have
does	for	who	said	what
you	two	that	where	says

Getting Stronger: Vowels (C)
Rhyme Time

Choose a word from the box that rhymes with the underlined word in each sentence. Write the word.

wig	chin	quick
pen	fox	sock

1. See the <u>cat</u>. It has a ___**hat**___.

2. Chad got a <u>rock</u>. It is in his _____.

3. I have a <u>hen</u>. It is in a _____.

4. Rex can <u>dig</u>. He gets a _____.

5. The can is <u>tin</u>. It hit my _____.

6. This is <u>Rick</u>. He is _____.

7. What is in the <u>box</u>? Is it a _____?

Endings –*ff*, –*ll*, and –*ss*
Color the Pairing Letters

Touch and say the sounds in the word.
Draw a square around the double letter endings.

1. b o s s

2. k i s s

3. m i s s

4. c u f f

5. p u f f

Just for Fun ....

Nonsense word:

s h i f f

Ending –all
Different Beat

Read each word in the row aloud. Circle the word in the row that does **not** rhyme with the others.

1. fall   ball   call   (Jack)

2. hall   Jill   mall   tall

3. falls   calls   hill   balls

In order, write each word you circled on the blank lines in the sentence. Read the sentence aloud.

4. _____ and _____

went up the _____ .

Introduce Compound Words
By Sight

Reading across the rows, see how many words you can
read correctly in one minute. When you get to the bottom
of the page, start over.

Mr.	my	why	she	with
your	their	went	they	of
from	have	he	to	and
Mrs.	are	one	her	or
so	want	we	both	put
Dr.	were	does	for	who
said	what	you	two	that

Practice Compound Words (B)
Match It

Draw a line from the sentence to the matching picture.

1. Rick is in the bathtub. •

2. A bobcat is not a pet. •

3. Does he huff and puff uphill? •

4. Where is my backpack? •

5. The eggshell is not red. •

Getting Stronger: Punctuation and Capitalization

Just Right!

Put a period or question mark at the end of the sentence.
Read the sentence aloud.

1. Will Jack kiss his fish _____

2. Is that a pig in the pigpen _____

3. That hotrod is quick _____

4. I cannot see the mess _____

5. Jess had fun with pinball _____

PHONICS

Getting Stronger: Endings –*ff*, –*ll*, –*ss*, –*zz*, and –*all*

Finish the Job

Choose a word from the box to complete the sentence.
Write the word. Read the sentence aloud.

gull	toss
fuzz	puff

1. There is _____ on the rug.

2. A _____ is on the dock.

3. Jill can _____ the ball to Ross.

4. I huff and _____ when I run uphill.

Read and Write Words
Word Chains

One letter has been changed to make the next word.
Color the box that has the changed letter.

j	a	m
y	a	m
h	a	m
h	a	t
h	u	t
h	u	g
b	u	g
b	i	g

w	i	g
w	i	n
p	i	n
p	e	n
p	e	t
p	o	t
d	o	t

Create Words

Dissect It

Find the words that begin with *th–*, *sh–*, *ch–*, or *wh–* in the sentence. Write the words.

1. Did you see that sunset? _____**that**_____

2. Mom will shut off the tap. _____

3. The hut has thick walls. _____

4. When did you get a cat? _____

5. You can chop a log with an ax. _____